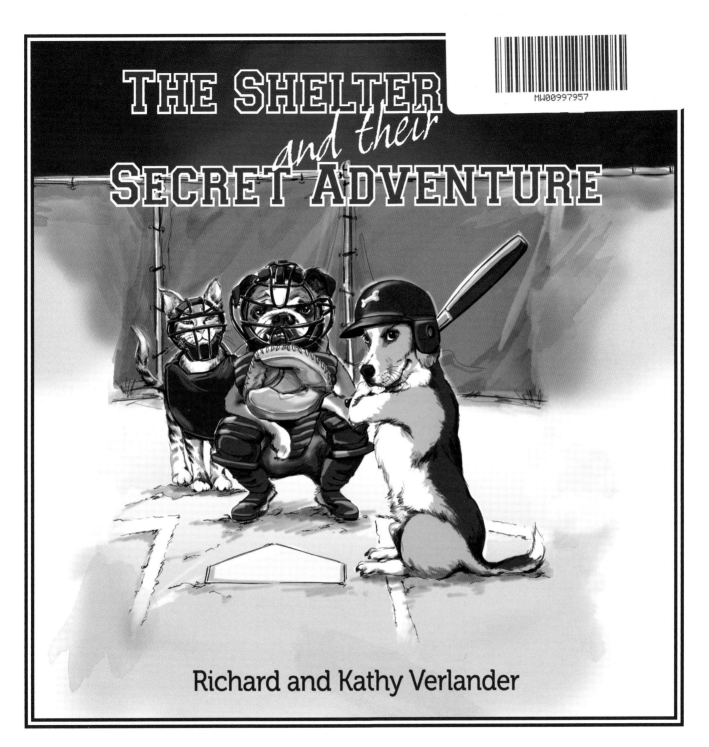

THE SHELTER
and their
SECRET ADVENTURE

Richard and Kathy Verlander

Authors
Richard and Kathy Verlander

Illustrator
David Pfendler

ISBN: 978-0-9992891-1-2

Cover Design and Page Layout
Jayne E. Hushen

Publisher
Wayne Dementi
Dementi Milestone Publishing, Inc.   Manakin-Sabot, VA 23103
www.dementimilestonepublishing.com

Printed in the USA

Dedication

This book is dedicated to all of those who give time and provide shelter to homeless animals. Your compassion and caring for those who solely depend upon us for their well being, with nothing to give but love in return, are an inspiration to all of us.

LIVE. LOVE. ADOPT.

About The Authors

Richard and Kathy Verlander are retired and live in rural Goochland, Va. They have two grown children and share an abiding love for kids, dogs, baseball, and all things outdoors. The Verlanders are also the adoptive parents of three dogs who qualify as family.

This is their second book. The first, *Rocks Across The Pond,* chronicles their fascinating journey raising MLB super star Justin Verlander and his younger brother Ben.

Richard and Kathy currently serve as volunteer campaign co-chairs with Goochland Pet Lovers, a non profit group that is raising funds to help with the construction of a new animal shelter in their hometown.

They volunteer at the shelter and love walking the dogs.

Table of contents

Chapter 1

"The Breakout!"

Beagles are escape artists. Everybody knows that....
So it should come as no surprise that each night after
Julie closes the door and clicks the lock at the animal
shelter, Barney is the first one out. In fact sometimes his
teammates call him "Houdini," although he doesn't know
why. What he DOES know is that humans are silly to think
he can't escape from his pen after they leave.

"It's so easy!!!"

What everyone DOESN'T know is that beagles are also very good baseball players! Barney is in fact the star short-stop on the animal shelter team. W-H-A-A-A-T??? Didn't know about the team? Or that dogs even played baseball?

Keep reading.....

You see, life at the shelter gets boring sometimes and the animals often get sad and lonely after their human friends leave for the night. They all wish they had forever homes to go to like them... Luckily, there is a baseball field right down the road from here, and most nights they sneak out to go play BASEBALL.

Before the group can start down the trail to the ball-park, Barney has to let his other friends out of their pens as well, and that includes the CATS! Since he started playing ball, Barney has learned that when it comes to cats you shouldn't just listen to what the dogs have to say... In fact, he actually likes his feline friends. They don't smell like the dogs sometimes do, and it turns out they can really play ball!

Chapter 2

"The Moonlight Trail"

So here they are, our furry little band of ballplayers sneaking out the back door of the shelter to start their nightly adventure. Titan, the German shepherd, leads them into the darkness and out onto the trail. Why not Barney you wonder? Well, as good as beagles are at escaping and playing shortstop, it turns out they are not the best at leading a group on a journey, even a short one...

They are always wandering off and constantly stop to sniff everything!

Titan is a great leader. His ancestors were guard dogs and this comes in handy when leading a march through the woods at night. Titan only has three legs, because while he was lost and trying to find his way home, he got hit by a car. Lucky for him the animal protection officers rescued him from the side of the road and took him to Dr. Lori. Dr. Lori is a veterinarian who volunteers at the shelter.

Titan thinks she and all of the other humans who work at the shelter are real heroes!

The moon shines brightly as our merry group of friends continue down the path. As they hustle along through the cool night air trying to keep pace with Titan, who is very fast for only having three legs, they pass behind a fenced-in area with huge containers and bins. It's a noisy place in the daytime and sometimes the banging sounds wake them from their afternoon naps at the shelter. All of the dogs have heard that this was a great place to visit when there was trash everywhere and it was called a dump.
Now the humans call it a "convenience station," but it's not nearly as much fun since it's not as smelly and dirty as before.

All at once the path opens onto a playground with swing sets, see saws, picnic shelters, and a concession stand. Off in the distance they can see their destination.... the baseball fields!!!! The group quickens their pace in anticipation of another night of fun playing their favorite game. As they approach the ballpark, Riley, who is a hound mix and is the best digger you ever saw, has already scratched a hole in the hard red clay beneath the outfield fence. Covered in dirt that nicely matches his reddish fur, he squeezes through and runs as fast as he can to open the main gate. Large dogs and a few others who might have eaten too many peanut butter treats at the shelter are too big to crawl under. (People who come to visit are always sneaking in food.)

The cats of course simply jump right over!

Now as you probably know, cats are way more nimble than dogs and can squeeze into just about anything. So, slipping into the equipment shed was no problem for Cleo the calico cat. It also helps that she is slim and trim. As it turns out, cats also make great umpires because they can see EVERYTHING!

Chapter 3

"The Big Game"

    The ballplayers quickly run into the dugouts where they pick up bats and gloves and get ready for the big game. Cleo is the umpire for tonight and as she waits beside home plate, Zoey, who is a Louisiana leopard dog, warms up to pitch. Barney the beagle scampers out to shortstop and gives a few short barks of encouragement to his team-mates. Sometimes if there's a great play made in the field, or someone gets a big hit, Beauregard the basset hound will actually start howling. Everyone then has to remind him to "tone it down" so he doesn't wake up the neighbors. The lights are usually on when they get to the field, (although no one has figured out why) and once the game begins they quickly start to have fun!

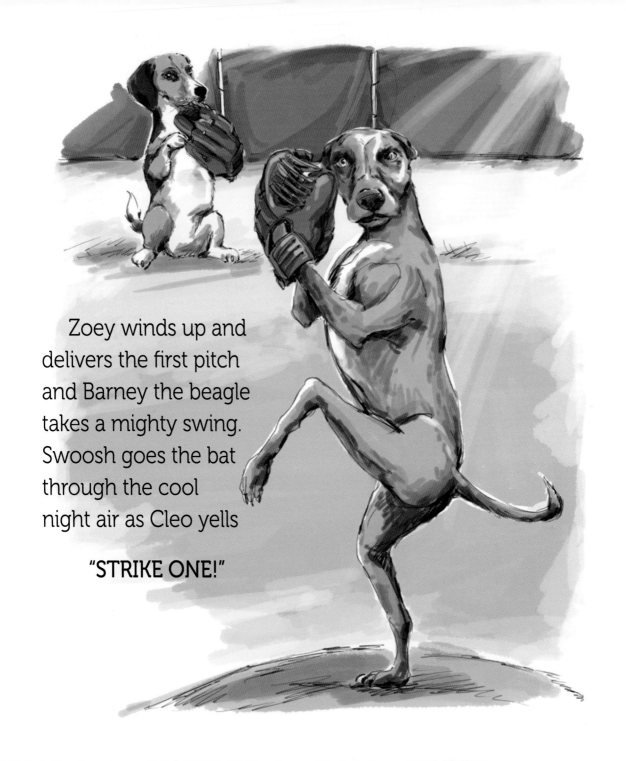

Zoey winds up and
delivers the first pitch
and Barney the beagle
takes a mighty swing.
Swoosh goes the bat
through the cool
night air as Cleo yells

"STRIKE ONE!"

Curtis, who is a yellow lab, goes charging home from his position at first base. Retrievers make great defenders, although sometimes his teammates have to remind him not to chase EVERY ball, just the ones that get hit in his direction.

The game goes on... the 2nd pitch and this time Barney doesn't miss. At the crack of the bat the ball sails high into right field where Bailey, (or "Miss B" as she is known to her friends) makes a nice catch on the warning track for out number one. Bailey is great at catching fly balls. She is part bird dog and loves to keenly watch the ball as it flies high in the sky, just like a real bird. Beauregard howls his approval from left field. Beau is not very fast, but he has a real nose for the ball.

Boomer the pit bull plays centerfield. Sometimes he makes great plays, but when the ball is hit to him he doesn't always throw to the correct base. As a matter of fact, he often just keeps the ball in his mouth and runs around in circles. Once in awhile, this makes his team-mates angry, but usually they just laugh because it's hard to be mad at Boomer. He loves everybody! Boomer is sad sometimes because people think he's mean because of the kind of dog he is. He has been at the shelter for a long time.

His teammates wish people would get to know him better.

Chapter 4

"The Storm Rolls In "

As the game rolls along, storm clouds gather and a few drops of rain start to fall. No one seems to notice until a big clap of thunder is heard and a flash of lightning lights up the dark night sky beyond the outfield fence. Quite a few of the ballplayers panic, and all at once there is a great rush toward the dugouts as a downpour begins! Lots of pushing and shoving can be seen and everyone is fighting for cover. Suddenly a loud bark booms across the infield,

"BREAK IT UP!" says Lucy...

Lucy, who is an Australian shepherd, hates it when someone gets out of line. Her ancestors were working dogs that were used to herd cattle and sheep and so Lucy knows a thing or two about how to get everyone rounded up in a hurry. She quickly takes charge and hustles the players off the field and into the dugout. Everyone huddles along the back wall, but this still doesn't completely protect them from the storm. The thunder cracks louder and the rain comes down in sheets.

Everyone is afraid and worries about how they will get back to the shelter...

Suddenly the beam of approaching headlights cuts through the night and a big blue truck can be seen circling the parking lot. Though the rain is still pouring, the group immediately recognizes the animal control vehicle...

"It's Officer Eric!" yells Barney, "someone run for help!!!"

Roxy is an older girl with lots of gray in her muzzle, but boy can she run! (The card on her kennel reads "greyhound mix.") Long and lean, she takes off like a bullet through the stormy night in pursuit of the truck. Eric is an animal control officer at the shelter and has rescued many of the group from some pretty scary situations in the past, so maybe he can help tonight.

Chapter 5

"The Rescue"

Sure enough, the officer sees Roxy coming. As soon as he slows the big truck down, Roxy quickly turns and runs back toward the ballpark. "This dog needs help," he thinks... So he steps on the gas and tries to keep up, following Roxy across the baseball field.

"WHAT IS GOING ON HERE????"

What happens next is something Eric won't soon forget... As he brings the truck to a stop and jumps out into the stormy night he is nearly bowled over by what seems like a whole shelter full of dogs and cats.

"Wait!

It is a shelter full!" Eric thinks . "OUR shelter!" Quickly the whole team loads into the back of the truck, pushing, shoving, soaking wet, but mostly just happy to be getting out of the storm.

The ride back to the shelter is short and it's a good thing because Officer Eric had to use the front and the back seat to carry everyone. As the truck rolls slowly back up the road, a great many paws, noses, and tails can be seen hanging out from all directions.

Harley, the boxer, can be seen sitting in the front seat beside Eric.

Chapter 6

"Trouble At The Shelter"

Officer Eric loves his job at the shelter. He also loves baseball... As a matter of fact, sometimes he goes to see games at the high school just down the road from the shelter. A couple of the players there have made it all the way to the big leagues!

And the team mascot is a Bulldog!

The gang gets a stern lecture when they are back at the shelter, safe and sound in their kennels. "You guys are going to get me in trouble sneaking out of here like this!" the officer says... But everyone notices he can't stop smiling. Winston, the Lhasa Apso, who is a terrible gossip, has heard a rumor that Eric is the one who is turning the lights on at the baseball field!!!!

Exhausted from their big night, everyone quickly falls asleep in their shelter beds. They dream of one day playing ball with families of their own. Curtis the lab snores loudly, but no one hears.

The rain outside has stopped.

Chapter 7

"The Next Day"

Morning comes early at the shelter and most days everyone is already up when Julie unlocks the front door and rushes in to say good morning and take everyone for a walk. This morning something is different though, as the animals also hear another familiar voice... It's Officer Tim! "Uh-oh," says Barney,

"I hope this isn't about last night..."

Officer Tim, you see, is the officer in charge of the shelter. While he's a nice man, he also has to be notified whenever someone gets in trouble. So now everyone is worried about sneaking off last night and having to be rescued from the storm! Just then Officer Tim shouts, "EVERYONE OUTSIDE AND INTO THE TRUCKS!"

"UH-OHHH !!!"

Before anyone knows what's going on, the shelter animals are loaded up and headed down the road. "Hey," says Curtis the lab, "we are going to the baseball field!" Now they really fear the worst. "Did Officer Eric tell on us?"

"Did we break something or dig too many holes?" "Did we leave in such a hurry that we left a mess?" A sign at the field says, "always leave the dugout cleaner than you found it."

Chapter 8

"Opening Day"

It was about then that they saw the balloons, and the signs, and all of the children in their uniforms lined up and down both sides of the baseball diamond. Good smells were coming from the grills outside the concession stand, and there was great excitement in the air. It was opening day at the Little League.

But what really got the team excited was there was also an adoption event for rescue animals...

"HEY! THAT'S US!"

Excitement builds as the animals jump out of the trucks and their human friends attach them to their leads. Harley the boxer is the first one out. He's followed by a pit bull named Bodie, and his inseparable companion Honeybee, a Jack Russell terrier.

Little children and their parents rush over to say hello. There is a great deal of tail wagging, wet kisses, and belly rubbing. Once the animals are led into their crates along the outside of the ball field, Julie attaches little signs to each pen. This is important because it tells people all about how special and different each animal is and how they might fit into their family.

And there were LOTS OF FAMILIES COMING BY!!!! Along with the smell of hamburgers on the grill, anticipation fills the air. "Everyone try not to bark or howl" says Officer Tim, but it's SOOO hard not to.
"It's going to be a great day!"

And what a day it was...

By the time the last games were ending and it started getting dark, the crates were all empty... As far as adoption events go it was a first. Never before had every animal found a forever home in a single day! But then there just seemed to be something magical about this place, and these pets.

As Officer Eric drives off in his truck, he smiles to himself and thinks how happy he and the rest of the staff are for all of their furry friends. They would sleep with their new families tonight.

And as we all suspected, Eric knew about the shelter team all along; and he would really miss the baseball game every night...

Chapter 9

"Homes Sweet Homes"

Later that night...

    As Barney the beagle closes his eyes to fall asleep, he thinks how wonderful it is to be part of a new family. He is already in love with the two boys named Justin and Ben, and feels right at home in his new bed. They made it just for him! His tail REALLY starts wagging when he notices all of the bats, gloves, and balls scattered around the boys' room.

        This was a baseball family!!!

As he finally drifts off, he dreams
of endless summer days
on the field. Days spent
retrieving ground balls at
shortstop, barking happily, and
growing up together with his
new teammates in his forever home.

The Real Players

BARNEY

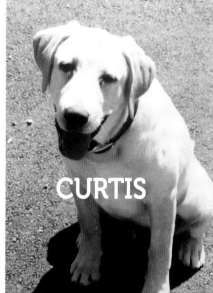

CURTIS

BAILEY

HARLEY

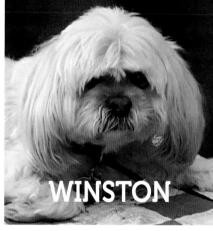

WINSTON

ZOEY

BOOMER

RILEY

LUCY

ROXY

TITAN

ERIC

HONEYBEE

BEAUREGARD

JULIE • TIM • LORI

CLEO

BODIE

Kathy
and
one of her shelter friends